JAMES LUGO'S
VOCAL
INSANITY

DISCOVER THE KEY TO UNLOCK THE DOOR TO AN INSANE VOCAL TONE

I0211234

Vendera
Publishing

Interior Design: Daniel Middleton
www.scribefreelance.com

Cover Design: Molly Burnside
www.crosssidedesigns.com

Produced by Jaime Vendera
Photography: James Lugo
Photo Detail:Travis Schlauderaff
All Audio Files: Recorded by James Lugo

ISBN: 978-1-936307-25-8

Printed in the United States of America

Contents

WELCOME TO VOCAL INSANITY. My name is James Lugo. I'll be your "singing" psychiatrist during this guided journey. Once you've been committed to my method of singer's shock therapy, ingested my approach to vocal technique and succumbed to my exercise regimen, your voice will be well on its way to becoming truly insane! If you want a crazy amazing voice, you must be prepared to think outside the box, no matter how nuts it may seem. So, be prepared for a mind-melting vocal experience. Before we slip into the musician's straight jacket, you must commit the Vocal Insanity motto to memory.

If you want to sing like a star you need to train like a star.

Whether you're singing in a church choir, belting it out in the garage with your buddies, gigging on the weekends, recording your first demo, or you're a touring/recording pro, the only way to stay on top of your game is to think and practice like you've already reached the top and plan to stay there! Why? Because you must be prepared for the demands required from your voice before you reach the top. I know firsthand and I've seen firsthand how singing on the road can send the unprepared vocalist back to their day job.

As a rock singer, no coach ever warned me about the rigorous demands of touring. In their defense, they didn't know. They were teachers, not singers, and simply didn't have the personal experience. I had no idea I'd be dealing with smoke, crappy food, poor ventilation, lack of sleep and loud stage volume. The art of singing is a craft that can be affected by many outside sources. Heed my advice; if you want to be a rock star, you best master your craft, because there's nothing more beneficial to your career than developing your instrument, understanding what can negatively affect that instrument, and mastering the true art of singing.

The true art of singing comes from singing, not from studying the epiglottis sphincter. I believe the analytical approach to vocal coaching creates a methodology, which only helps build a house that no one will ever want to buy. By developing a contrived sound through a methodology designed to increase your physical/mechanical knowledge as opposed to singing knowledge, you'll lose the passion and artistic nature of the primal sound.

I don't believe in methods that force you to manipulate your tone in order to sound like everybody else. We're all unique, so let me show you how to sound like you. The method that I teach is focused on building an amazing sound by enhancing your own natural tone without manipulating your voice to sound like your favorite singer.

My approach is the same method that allowed me to tour with the Manny Charlton Band (the original guitarist and songwriter for Nazareth.) Our gigs required me to sing all the Nazareth hits, including "Love Hurts" and "Hair of the Dog" in their original key. I was able to capture Dan McCafferty's unique sound, while maintaining my own natural tone.

Many singers, especially without proper training, attempt to mimic the singer they are covering. Mimicking can be vocally damaging, which is why I'm against the contrived sound methods. My method of vocal insanity allows singers to unlock a powerful, refined voice, without losing the raw urban tone that *sells* records.

What's the secret? It's the same secret that singers of bands like Led Zeppelin, Guns N' Roses, Whitesnake and more have used to release 'out of this world' tones that have produced hit after hit for over the past 40 years. The secret is building an intense *pharyngeal voice.* The pharyngeal voice is that killer tone that lives between the chest and head voice. It is the key to hitting those piercing high notes that can peel the paint right off the walls and flesh off your face, all without losing your voice for days on end! It's that biting tone that sounds as if it's being produced somewhere between falsetto and full voice, but with balls.

When I started to unlock the pharyngeal voice in my own singing, I was suddenly able to easily sing songs I could have never imagined singing in the past. Once I was able to figure out a way to transmit this stunning revelation to others, I began to see miracles happen for my students; miracles that were nothing short of amazing. I witnessed singers who could barely hit a G above middle C suddenly living their dreams, singing Soundgarden and Kelly Clarkson with ease. The pharyngeal voice IS the secret. However, it is the area of the voice that most singers lack and the main focus for this book. And now that you have had a taste of what lies ahead in my method of madness, I invite you all into the Vocal Asylum.

DISCLAIMER: The following sections are not intended to prescribe, treat, prevent, or diagnose any illness. Consult your physician before attempting any exercises listed in this book.

Chapter One: Breathing

MY OBJECTIVE IN WRITING THIS BOOK is to take what I've learned over the years and make the process of singing simple by exploring the concepts and techniques of singing pop and rock, while covering intricate topics pertinent to voice. The best place to start is with breathing because your breath is your singing fuel. Without fuel, your ride is over...So, Here we go!

Let's start with a simple question. Why are babies so loud? Give up? Babies are free to make noise because they haven't been taught the meaning of being forced to "shut-up". Babies are yet to have truck payments, pushy bosses or traffic to contend with. So what do babies have to do with singing? Everything! Babies are natural born wailers. They're loud because they're free. By not being conditioned by society, (yet) a baby's natural innocence and ignorance to volume allows the baby's cry to be naturally intense. No one has told the baby to be quiet; not to the baby's knowledge anyway.

Singers struggle because they've forgotten how to be as vocally free as when they were lying in the crib. Can you honestly say you've heard a baby lose their voice from crying? No, you say? I'm betting you can name a dozen singers who've gone hoarse even after a few songs, blaming it on everything from a cold, to caffeine, to not being in the zone. While these things do have some validity, nine times out of ten, it's due to lack of vocal freedom. We've lost our freedom, but now it's time to get it back...and it starts with studying the baby cry...

Why exactly are babies loud, beyond the psychologically obvious? Simple; it's the pharyngeal tone. The baby has not stood upright yet, so the spinal erector muscles are not fully developed. Therefore, they are free to wail by using the abdominal muscles, which are not bogged down by simple acts such as walking and sitting. This plays a huge role in the cutting tone that escapes an infant's mouth while crying.

And crying, my friend, is a pure, free-flowing tone.

That type of free-flowing tone is the same sound you hear when you listen to the voices from bands like Linkin Park, Foo Fighters, and Soundgarden, as well as singers like Kelly Clarkson, Christina Aguilera, Mary J. Blige, Katy Perry, and Martina McBride. This is the sound we are looking to produce in pop and rock; raw, uninhibited rage! That my friend is the commonality between the baby's voice and what we are trying to establish as singers.

If we can't transmit to the ears of the outside world the tone and emotion we mentally hear on the inside, we'll be waiting tables instead of performing! This is especially true of Rock, R&B, Hip-Hop and Hardcore vocals. Thin and wimpy voices need not apply. You've got to put muscle in that voice to make your plea come to life and touch those people in the back row of your audience. If you're ready to put some high-octane leaded fuel in those pipes and live out your dreams, read on.

Back to the baby... Because the baby is relaxed, the body functions naturally. As the baby breathes, air appears as if it is inhaled into the lower belly. Just watch as a baby inhales and exhales while he or she is lying on their back. It's amazing. The lower abdominal region rises and falls naturally, which is the way adults breathe while sleeping.

Many singers today have forgotten this way of breathing, taking shallow breaths by lifting the shoulders and puffing out the chest. This is called chest breathing and causes vocal strain and lack of range. Chest breathing is a controlled reaction we've learned from watching others.

It's funny to think that once we fall asleep and we no longer maintain conscious control of our bodies that we revert to natural breathing. In order to be at the top of your game as a singer, you must regain your natural breathing pattern by breathing low and deeply to establish the power source which will fuel your voice and release vocal tension. The origin of the baby's voice is very low, meaning that the baby breathes very deeply.

If you want to rock, it's time to revisit your past. The best way to do it without climbing into a crib is to lie down on the ground on your back, stick a book on your belly (preferably this one) and begin inhaling/exhaling. As you inhale, the book should rise, and it should fall as you exhale. Does it feel funny? Tough...Live it, learn it, love it! It's the only way to breathe to fill the tank and give you that high-octane fuel you'll need for singing powerful tunes.

Inhale   **Exhale**

Deep, low breathing is the key to power and learning how to project a more powerful sound without blowing up your instrument. FYI—YOU ARE YOUR INSTRUMENT! If you want to understand more about how to project a larger sound, think of yourself as an acoustic guitar. An acoustic guitar is an enclosed chamber with a hole in it. People are enclosed chambers with a mouth. Keeping that in mind, the bigger the chamber, the bigger the sound, which means the deeper you use your breathing chamber, the greater the sound will be that you produce! Remember, just as the larger guitar has a more resonant sound, the singer can increase the size of the chamber by breathing deeper into the lower belly.

Still having trouble with this way of breathing? Think of inhaling like filling up a glass of water from the faucet. You put the glass under the spout and it fills from the bottom up. As you inhale, imagine pouring the air into the very bottom of your lungs and filling them up to the top with air. Filling from the bottom up is the secret to a loud, powerful voice. Get loud? What a concept! After everything you've learned over the years about being quiet and sucking in your stomach, as singers, we're going back to being natural breathers and naturally resonant.

Because of societal stresses, being told to shut up and stand upright as a child, you've more than likely developed the chest breather's habit of shallow breathing. This is very bad for singers and can result in vocal suicide. Your voice resonates to a great degree in your chest and body. This means that the notes vibrate and the sound is accentuated within your chest. If you find that you are shallow breathing, you're stifling the natural resonance and selling your voice short. You will not be able to pour out your full potential to your audience until you breathe deeply and fully into your belly.

Shallow breathing can lead to over-singing to compensate for a small sound, which in turn can lead to vocal problems. In other words, you'll end up pushing or squeezing with the stomach, clenching in the throat, and shouting to reach those high notes. You might notice when you add this much stress to make a powerful sound that you end up making faces that would make Joe Walsh blush; causing the veins in your neck to look like they're about to burst through your skin.

All these factors will overwork the vocal cords. Trust me; you don't want to start having vocal cord problems, because they are unforgiving, kind of like skydiving. Yeah, you may survive if your chute doesn't open, but that's a big if. The vocal cords are delicate. Once they are damaged, they cannot regenerate the way other areas of the body do, so there's not a lot of room for error. Serious vocal cord damage could result in requiring surgery to fix the mess, which can further result in loss of that amazing tone you once possessed. The key to saving your voice is to relax, breathe deep, and let your belly drop slightly as you inhale. When you do this, you will lower the origin of your voice and begin to improve your sound.

Breathing is where it begins, so it's training time. Here are the top *Vocal Insanity* exercises for breathing, and yes, I do them…

Exercise #1 - Lying 10's — I affectionately refer to this exercise as the "Granny Exercise." If you've ever had a singing lesson with one of those nice, old ladies who use to teach choir-you know the type-out of tune, upright piano, ten cats, and she won't let you leave until you've had some cookies. This exercise is the first thing she has you do, and for a good reason. It works!

Lie on the floor on your back and relax. Leave your problems and your intellect at the door, because you won't need them. They'll only get in the way. Put a book on your lower stomach, directly on or slightly below your belly button. Slowly and evenly breathe, focusing on the book rising when you inhale and lowering as you exhale. Do this several times to get the rhythm. Yes, this sounds familiar considering I've already had you on the floor with this book on your belly, so now we'll take it up a notch.

When you feel comfortable with the rhythm of the book rising and falling, begin timing the flow of your breathing. Inhale slowly and evenly for ten seconds, hold your breath for ten seconds, and then exhale slowly and evenly for ten seconds.

Sound easy? For some people it will be. It will seem very natural. For others, it will take some effort. Regardless, this is a very important exercise, so don't skip it or you'll never become vocally insane.

Seconds count, so make sure it takes the entire ten seconds to inhale. A few seconds before the end of the inhalation cycle, you want the chest to expand slightly, but not so much as to create a feeling of constriction in the throat or chest. When holding your breath for ten seconds, don't lock your throat like grunting, or you will feel throat tension. Focus on the sensation as if you are still inhaling to hold the breath as opposed to blocking air release with the vocal cords. As you release the breath, lower the book slowly and evenly for ten seconds. Toward the end of the movement, your chest should lower and you should feel empty of air. The key to this movement is consistency. As you progress with this exercise, you can increase the time to fifteen seconds each, twenty seconds each, and so on. Let's move on.

Exercise #2 - Butterfly Wings — This is a very cool and relaxing exercise - so enjoy it. Stand up and put your feet about shoulder width apart. Place your hands down by your sides and begin to inhale.

As you slowly inhale, begin to bring your arms out to your sides, extending up and over your head.

Make sure you feel as if you're breathing down into your belly when you inhale, like filling a glass of water. DON'T GET RIGID when you do this exercise! Relax and feel the air rush into the lower abdomen. This is very natural if you just let go!

At the top of the movement, your hands will reach the highest point and you will be filled with air. Hold the stretch, trying to touch the sky.

I like to put my head back, open my mouth as wide as I can and stick my tongue out as far as it will go at the top of the inhale.

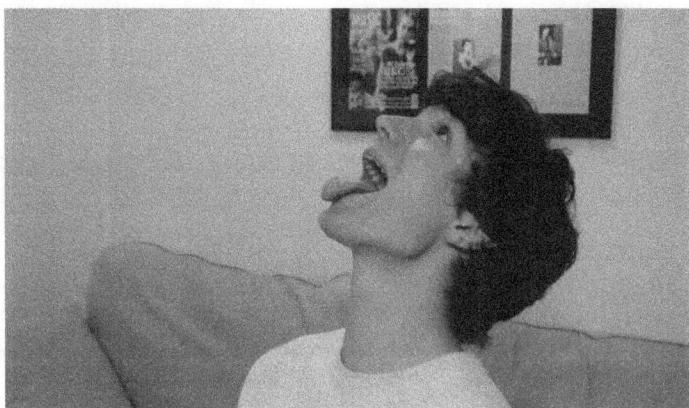

Think *Steven Tyler*...
BIG OPEN MOUTH FOR AN AMAZINGLY HUGE SOUND!

You'll notice a relaxed sensation in your mouth, especially the palate, (the roof of your mouth) as well as in the neck when you tilt your head back and open your mouth. This is that freedom sensation that must exist when the sounds float out of your mouth.

Back to breathing- Once you feel the air in the lower stomach, begin slowly exhaling while lowering your arms.

WOW, big head rush! Be careful not to lose your balance. Now that you're buzzing, let's try another breathing exercise.

Exercise #3 - Compression Lung Expansion – I must preface this technique by mentioning that this exercise is one of the best movements for increasing lung capacity. Be careful not to overdo it if you have a weak back. The purpose of this movement, as its name indicates, is to expand your lungs. After years of shallow breathing, a singer can no longer access the lower aspect of the lungs for singing. It is said that the lungs can become somewhat deformed at the bottom, impeding the elasticity that allows the lungs to fill to full capacity. The following exercise will stretch out the lungs and begin to allow you to reach your true oxygen potential.

Remember - big air, big voice, big fat paycheck!

OK here we go! Put your hands up high above your head and fill your lungs ALL the way up with air.

Think of filling them like a glass of water, from the bottom-up. When your lungs are completely filled with air, slowly begin to lower your arms over in front of you as you bend at the waist.

Attempt to touch your toes, while holding your breath. Try to keep the legs straight if it's comfortable. If they bend slightly at the knees, that's okay too.

If you can't go all the way down, don't force it. Only stretch as far as comfortably possible. After several weeks of this exercise, you'll become more limber and be able to touch your toes. When you've reached as far as you can in the stretch, wiggle your butt and continue to hold your breath. You will feel the lungs and ribs expand. After ten seconds or so, come up slowly as you exhale slowly and evenly.

This exercise can make you feel a bit spacey. Don't let the dizziness alarm you. You're forcing oxygen into places that have probably needed it for a long time. Your body has learned to cope with a lack of oxygen and now it must cope with a better oxygenation level.

These three exercises work well together and should be done every day before you begin your main vocal exercises and/or singing. Start by doing them for approximately five minutes for each exercise per day. Increase the amount of time for each movement as necessary.

The final segment in the breathing section is stretching. After performing the three breathing exercises, it's a good idea to release tension in the body. The military taught me a great way to stretch, which was releasing tension "from the top to the bottom". While you stretch, make sure you are breathing deeply, slowly, and evenly. A good rule of thumb during the stretch is to be sure all the air is exhaled out of your body as you reach the apex of each stretch, but don't hold your breath. Deeply inhale as you come out of the stretch. Use the following pictures and descriptions as your guideline:

With legs straight, lift one arm behind you to the ceiling and the other arm down to the opposite foot for a full body stretch.

Come to the center and hang head to the floor.

Lean backward. Keep breathing!

Extend one arm straight, bringing it to the opposite side as the opposite hand pulls to stretch the upper arm and shoulder.

Lean the neck to the left, then right to gently stretch the neck and shoulder.

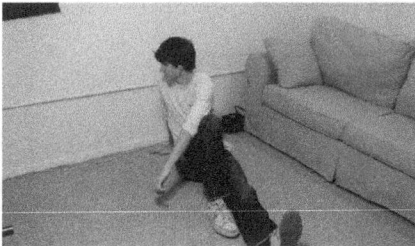

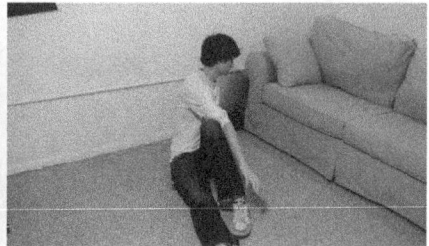

Move to the floor, extend one leg and raise the opposite knee.
Rest the opposite arm across opposite knee and twist the body.

With legs extended from a sitting position, reach for the toes.

Leaning against a wall for support, extend one leg backward while bending
the other leg forward. Push back on your extended leg to stretch the calf muscle.

Extend the tongue for a tongue stretch.

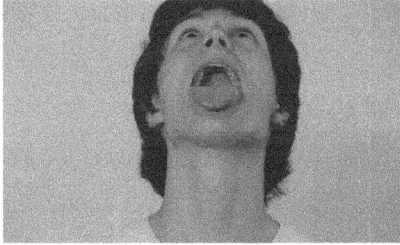

With tongue out, lean head back to stretch the throat.

If you followed along with the pictures, I'm betting you now feel great! Now that you're becoming a breathing animal, it's time to move on to discovering your voice. With that said, do **NOT** stop doing the breathing exercises and stretches! Perform them every day and as you learn new exercises in the following chapters, your daily routine will grow until you have a full-fledged vocal warm up/workout. Let's roll...

Chapter Two: Pure Vocal Function

NOW WE REACH THE MEAT AND POTATOES of this book, where the rubber meets the road, where you'll begin to understand pure vocal function. The term "pure vocal function" refers to the moment the vocal cords come together and form a seal. To get the full idea of what this means, let's start with the basics.

You have two vocal cords that sit horizontally in the mid-throat, known as the larynx. The vocal cords are closer together at the frontal aspect of the throat and V apart as they go back in the larynx towards the back of your neck when breathing. When vocalizing, the vocal cords come together. These vocal cords are approximately one half inch long and are made of material similar to ligament tissue. They have three muscles on either side that dovetail together, meaning they are connected, creating a seal where the vocal cords meet. The muscles are the Basic Muscle, Pharyngeal Muscle and Falsetto Muscle.

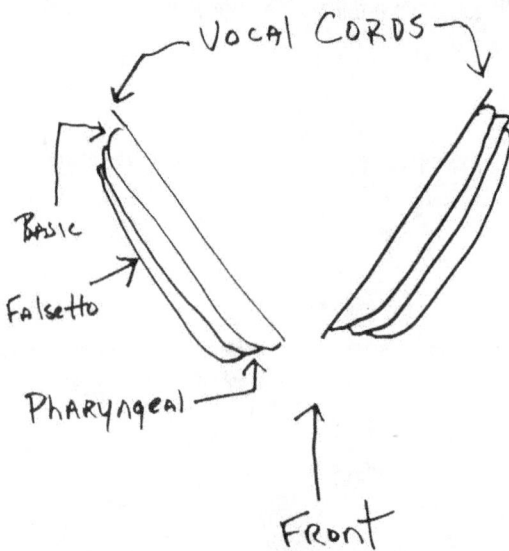

Here's a breakdown of each:

1. **Basic Muscle** — Also known as "Full Mechanism" or "Chest Voice." This muscle is the longest and thickest, creating a fat, beefy tone. This is your lower range and speaking voice.

2. **Pharyngeal Muscle** — Also known as the "Witches Cackle" or "Middle Voice." This muscle in thinner and shorter than the basic muscle and will help the vocal cords produce a higher pitch when contracted. It's very important to develop the pharyngeal muscle if you want to produce an intense crank in your voice, which is crucial for hard rock.

3. **Falsetto Muscle** — Also known as the "Flutter Muscle" because the vocal cords almost "flutter" because of the wide distance between them when engaging this muscle. This muscle is even shorter and thinner than the pharyngeal muscle and will contract to the highest notes in a singer's range. Many use falsetto because they haven't developed the ability to sing higher in their true voice due to lack of pharyngeal muscle development.

Knowing about these three muscles won't make you a better singer. Exercises that work all three muscles are the key. You don't have to be a watchmaker to own a watch. All you need is the ability to tell time. It has been my experience that some vocal instructional books are too wordy and detailed and all they ever did for me was take me away from my goal of understanding how the voice really works. All I wanted for myself as a vocal student were the tools to build a bulletproof voice! I spent a lot of years studying voice before a coach sat me down and explained in a simplistic way the truth of how the voice works.

Looking back, I believe that a lot of the vocal coaches I studied under may not have understood the basics of vocal mechanics themselves. But once I had an understanding, I realized that this knowledge was a vital aspect of my life as a singer and the bedrock upon which my vocal coaching was built. And it didn't require me studying to be an ENT! Like I said above, as one of my old teachers use to say, "You don't have to be a watchmaker to own a watch. You just need to know how to tell time."

To simplify vocal production, here's the stripped-down explanation of how you produce sound:

1. It starts with a signal sent from your brain telling your body it's time to sing.
2. Next, your diaphragm, the partition of muscle under the abdominal cavity, drops slightly, altering the air pressure in your lungs, allowing your lungs to fill with air. This should be natural, not forced. When you first begin to inhale by contracting the diaphragm, you'll notice there is some effort involved. Don't sweat it. After a few weeks it becomes second nature, because all you're doing is returning to the natural breathing pattern you were given at birth.
3. With your lungs filled with air, the vocal cords come together, creating a seal. It's very important that they come together to create the seal before you exhale and begin to sing. If you start to sing before the seal is made, you will hear a sound of rushing air mixed in with your voice. It will sound like you're using the "H" consonant at the beginning of everything you sing. This is known as aspiration. It's not good for your voice or the listener. If you are forcing the sound, it could also sound like an abrupt grunt or smack. This is what is known as a glottal shock. This is not to say you can't sing airy or add a little glottal shock now and then for effect, but if it's all you can do, it's very limiting, especially if a producer wants a solid note.

Another important thing to understand about aspiration is that it is similar to whispering, which is actually bad for the voice. It's great for the occasional effect in a song, but too much of it can cause the vocal cords to lose the seal that creates the compression needed for solid tone. As the vocal cords vibrate, they repeatedly hit each other. But this is not damaging if a proper seal is first created. Your job is to have the vocal cords sealed together as they begin to touch, not separated where they have more leverage that can lead to damage.

Here's a great analogy. Walk closely behind a horse. If he kicks you, you'll probably live. Walk a little farther behind the horse. If he kicks you, you'll probably die. Why? The distance creates a greater point of impact. Whispering is like walking farther behind the horse. The vocal cords whip against each other at a greater point of impact because there is a greater distance between the cords. If the seal is closed, you will produce pure sound without hiss. The seal created within the vocal cords during sound production without hiss is actually healthier for the voice.

Most people whisper when they have a sore throat. In reality, it's better not to speak at all rather than whisper. All in all, whispering can do lots of harm, causing the vocal cords to swell until they can't seal. Don't believe me? Take a look at your palms. These are your vocal cords. Now, smack your hands together over and over again as hard and fast as you can for ten seconds. Take a look at your now red palms. These are your vocal cords when whispering. Let's move on.

4. As you slightly tighten your belly and begin to exhale slowly and evenly, the air begins to buzz through the sealed vocal cords. This is similar to when you pull apart the end of balloon filled with air and it makes a squeaking sound. It is also similar to holding a reed of grass between your thumbs and blowing to create a whistle.

5. A sound beam comes off the vocal cords and rises up into the mouth and head region. Your vocal cords do not produce the voice you hear when a person sings because the vocal cords only buzz. The beautiful voice you hear is a product of the buzz resonating in the chest, head and face and the aperture of the mouth, which is used in forming the five primary vowels; EH, AH, EE, OH, OO.

When all these actions are put into motion, you are on your way to a better voice. Having a solid understanding of basic vocal function is one of the first steps in your journey to achieving your vocal and musical goals, and to getting that sound in your head out to the world. Now that you have a basic understanding of pure vocal function, let's move on to the next chapter where we'll develop a deeper understanding of your voice.

Chapter Three: Your Voice

NOW THAT YOU'VE GOT A HANDLE on breathing and how the vocal cords work, this section will explain the nuts and bolts of how your singing voice functions and what singing in a "blend voice" actually means.

First, let's look at range. You have both a low range and high range, or in singer's terms, two main registers in your voice. A register is a specific area of notes in your range, predetermined at birth that delegates where you can sing comfortably. Singers have a lower range, known as the "chest voice" and a higher range, known as the "head voice". This is a very simplistic outline, but stay with me on this.

Between the chest and head registers lies what is known as the *break*. The break is the point at which your voice cracks or makes a yodeling sound as you try to sing from the lower notes to the higher ones. The break creates many problems for singers and is the main reason the vocalist seeks coaching.

I have good news and bad news. The bad news is that your break will never go away because it isn't actually a break at all, but the transition point between that chest and head voice, or better put, a place where the vocal mechanism changes gears. The good news is that I'll teach you how sing through the so-called break without cracking, which will give you a seamless transition.

A seamless transition is just what it implies; a seamless voice able to sing from your lowest note to the highest note at the top of your range without struggling, breaking, or flipping into a wimpy falsetto. This seamless transition enables you to smoothly connect the low and high voice so that your range sounds flawless. By creating the seamless transition, you'll also increase your range...and those high notes are where the money is!

Why does the vocal break occur? Your voice cracks at the break because it shifts the workload abruptly from one muscle to the next. In other words, singing in your chest voice requires one specific muscle coordination, while singing in your head voice requires another. As you sing up a scale from your chest voice you will discover that at a certain note the muscles transition to cater to your higher head voice notes. Usually a man's voice will transition around E flat below High C and a woman's voice will transition at around B flat below High C. This is a general estimation but most of my students shift around there.

Your voice has a break for a very good reason. The break is a safety feature. Let's take a look at how pitch is made in order to get a better understanding of how the break works in your favor. Remember, your vocal cords have three muscles on either side of them-Basic, Pharyngeal and Falsetto. Pitch is increased or raised by the contraction of one or more of these muscles. The muscles contract like your bicep contracts as you strike a muscle pose.

As the vocal muscles contract, they stretch the vocal cords and the pitch goes higher, much like turning a tuning peg on a guitar; the tighter the string, the higher the note. If you tighten a guitar string too much, it will break. The same applies to your voice, but your vocal cords won't actually snap. That doesn't mean this over-stretching won't cause damage. You may fall victim to calluses on the cords, which are known as vocal nodules. In some cases this can lead to permanent voice loss.

The thing to understand about the three muscles along the outside of the vocal cords is that they are like the strings on a grand piano. If you open the top on a grand piano, you will notice that the longest, thickest strings are for the bass notes and as the piano notes go higher the strings get shorter and thinner. The lowest string is a thick, cable-like string that is six feet long. The highest string is thin, like a thread, and only six inches long.

The connection between the voice and the piano is simple. Long, thick piano strings will not tune up for the high notes, just as the long, basic muscle will not contract to create your upper register notes.

When you start singing in your chest voice, the basic muscle begins to contract to produce the lower notes. What creates the break is the abrupt shift from the basic muscle contraction to the falsetto muscle, which is now contracting to carry the workload. The quick change makes a "clunk" sound in your voice, because the long, thick basic muscle is much beefier sounding that the short, thin falsetto muscle. The key to creating the seamless transition across the break area is to use your pharyngeal muscle as a bridge, since it sits between the basic and falsetto muscle, so that your voice doesn't break and flip into falsetto.

Another contributing factor to the "clunk" sound includes a sudden shift where the note resonates. The lower notes resonate or vibrate in the chest, hence the name "chest voice" and the higher notes resonate in the head, hence the name "head voice." So, as your voice breaks up to the higher notes, it instantly shifts the resonation to the head. As it breaks back down into the lower register, it will shift back to chest resonation.

The chest is a larger resonating chamber than the head, which naturally creates a fuller sound. Without mastering how to create the blend between the basic and pharyngeal muscle, you'll always notice a huge difference in tone, have a continual break, and feel strain throughout the break area.

In summation, the break comes as the resonation shifts quickly from the full chest cavity to the smaller head chamber as the muscle coordination shifts abruptly from the fuller sounding basic muscle to the thinner falsetto muscle.

Now back to why this built-in safety feature is so important. Your voice has a break so that you can't contract the basic muscle so tight that you damage your voice. This doesn't mean that singers haven't tried. Many have and it resulted in vocal damage, which occurs when the basic muscle is contracted beyond its note range. If a singer continues to abuse the voice in this manner, it will lead to permanently damaging the vocal cords, possibly causing ruptures in the vocal cords called polyps, as well as causing vocal nodules. Nodules and polyps will keep the seal from, well, sealing.

All you need to know is that trying to sing too high in your chest register is bad. Singing too high in your chest voice is referred to as "pulling chest", "using too much weight" or "not honoring your bridge." I'm sure you've heard a singer who forced their voice up high and it sounded like they were shouting or straining. Maybe you knew them, and the very next day, they could barely speak. See my point? The cure to this ailment is, "Don't do it!"

So, how do you get the muscles to work correctly? No worries. In the audio portion of this instruction, I will be coaching you on how to strengthen your pharyngeal muscle and sing in a blend voice, which is a combination of head and chest voice created simultaneously. Speaking of the blend, let's jump to the next chapter...

Chapter Four: The Blend Voice

USING A BLEND VOICE LETS YOU sing through your complete range effortlessly. The blend voice also adds dimension to your voice by accessing more muscle contraction, allowing your voice to resonate in the head and chest cavities simultaneously.

The chest voice by nature resonates in the chest and has a thick sound, while the head voice resonates in the head and has a more bell-like or soaring sound. By using the blend, your voice resonates in both the head and chest and has a thick muscle sound that rings like a bell and soars...WOW! Can you spell $$$?

That's what I'm talking about when my students hear me talking about a *multi-dimensional voice*. The multi-dimensional voice accesses more muscle, more resonating space, creating a bigger, fuller, monstrous tone. This is one of the most important things for a singer to master. Now, I'll explain it in a simple way:

1. You have a chest voice that has a ceiling on it, which means it can only sing so high before the basic muscle has reached full contraction. If you're contracting the basic muscle too much, trying to sing too high using only the chest voice, you will start to sing flat and the note will start to have a loud, shouting, strained sound. Singing this way might even give you a sore throat.

2. Next, you have a head voice that will allow you to access the highest notes in your range, but the sound of the head voice in and of itself is thin and wimpy, because most singers using head voice are actually using falsetto.

3. Between the two voice registers you have the break where your voice shifts abruptly, making your voice sound unprofessional and weak. But remember, that break is there for a reason. It's a safety feature. Your voice will activate

the break when it can no longer sing in the chest voice, meaning you're going too high for the basic muscle to contract.

4.   The KEY to ultimate vocal freedom is to slowly and gradually bring in the properties of the head voice long before the break. To accomplish this, it must occur while still in chest voice, at which point, you start to allow the pharyngeal and falsetto muscles to contract, while maintaining the basic muscle contraction. As these other muscles start to contract, it allows your voice the ability to keep singing higher and higher without having to break. It also allows you to use some of the basic muscle all the way up to the top of your range. The basic muscle will keep the voice sounding beefy and full. As you gradually introduce the pharyngeal and falsetto muscles, you will not even hear any tone weakening and your voice will appear seamless, sounding like one voice.

So, how do you do this? It's very simple, but not always easy. As you practice every day with the audio section of *Vocal Insanity*, your voice will begin to adapt to this new way of singing. But there are many rules to follow, both when practicing and singing. As you begin to sing higher from your lower chest voice, you must:

1.   Keep your jaw loose, yet stable and stable and dropped at the hinge. The hinge is the point where the lower and upper jaw comes together in front of the ear... This allows the voice to come off the vocal cords

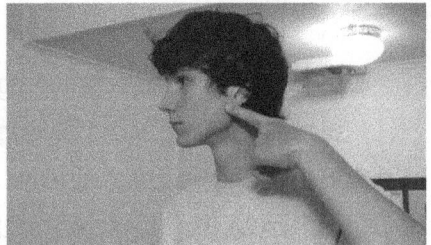

and out of the mouth correctly. Remember, when you listen to a song, whether it's Korn or Pink, all you're hearing is what that singer sounded like one inch off their mouths, which is approximately the size of a quarter (the size of a microphone diaphragm). It's very important that you get your voice moving with intensity to release it out of your mouth. Again, think of Steven Tyler.

2. Keep your tongue flat and forward in your mouth, resting the tip against the back of the bottom teeth. Flattening the tongue is very important as it helps to keep your larynx from jumping around

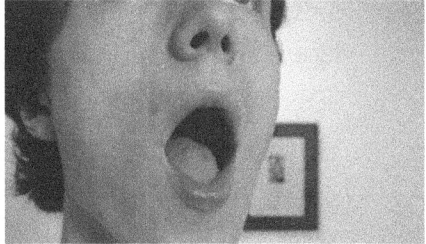

from low to high like a wild school girl. A crazy larynx can lead to vocal troubles, so let's nip it in the bud right now. Luckily, the flat tongue will keep the larynx in place as you start to add more intensity to your singing, or really "lean on" your voice.

3. Tighten the belly slightly as you sing. The abdominal muscles supports your voice much like the way a pillar supports an overhang. The pillar simply supports the overhang allowing the weight to rest down against it. It does not push it up. Pushing incorrectly too hard can damage your voice and cause throat problems. It's easiest to tighten by pushing down to tighten the stomach as if you were going to the restroom, which tightens the belly to support the voice.

4. As you go up in range, listen to the sound. You want the sound to start to move up and in slightly, like a steeple, as you sing higher. This means the tone of your voice needs to get a little thinner, warmer, and less trebly as you sing higher. What you want to avoid is that splatting "out of the mouth" singing tone that many new singers produce. For many people, this unpleasant shouting approach is an easy or "cheaters" way to extend their range without actually strengthening the instrument. Beyond the fact that this tone can possibly be causing vocal damage, it just doesn't sound too hot. This is best explained on the audio. The key is not to have the sound get brassy on the higher notes. If your voice sounds thin, strained, and brassy, it's a sign of pulling chest.

5. As you come back down the scale into chest voice, allow the head voice resonation to drop with it, returning to the same sound you started with. So, if we begin a scale starting on middle C and go up an octave, the sound, tone, and feeling on the low C note should return when we finish the scale.

6. VERY IMPORTANT! Understanding what makes us sing high is the foundation of this whole section. There are two contributing factors to why a person sings or even speaks high:

    A.   Emotion

    B.   Distance

Emotion: The more intense a person feels about something, the higher their voice will go to express that feeling. Listen to people talk when they get excited or scared. Their voice goes up in pitch. When people laugh, their voice can easily jump up an octave without even knowing. You'll notice that there is no effort on the part of the person to reach those higher notes when they are laughing or scared. The high notes occur with ease.

Distance: The farther someone is away from you, the higher the pitch is needed to call to them. Why? Because the higher registers carry farther. Talk to someone next to you and then call to someone across the street and you will see for yourself. Your pitch goes higher. When you must extend the voice over a distance, you subconsciously use the body to increase volume and range. Some call this "projection" or "projecting the voice."

To increase your range, you must combine the two contributing factors. From now on, when you sing or practice the vocal exercises from this book, I want you to imagine singing farther out or away from you as you slightly tighten your belly. This doesn't mean for you to yell and hurt your voice. It's about focusing your voice out away from you, while thinking, "sing farther" as you keep your belly tight with everything else in your body relaxed. In other words, relax your face, tongue, neck, shoulders and hands.

While you're relaxed, connect to your voice with emotion. Put plead in your voice; an unquenchable longing. Emotion IS the key. When you're singing a song, feel the words and respond accordingly. If the song is sad, happy, or angry, become sad, happy, or angry as you sing. While you do scales, do your best to place your mind on something that will fuel the intensity you need to hit those blistering high notes. After all, singing *is* method acting!

I know you are excited to get to the exercises. They will come soon enough. Once you start the vocal exercise routine, I suggest you reread this chapter to recap the essential points of singing. Let's move on to vowels, which are our keys to amazing tone.

Chapter Five: Primary Vowels

VOWELS PRODUCE YOUR TONE, plain and simple. It's the movement of the vowel that carries your voice and the words which you sing. You only sing vowels, not consonants. Listen to the radio. You'll notice that the singer will be singing the five primary vowels from the Latin tongue. The consonants only break up the melody and help form the sound of the words.

The Consonants are:

b, c, d, f, g, h, j, k, l, m, n, p, q, r, s, t, v, w, x, z

The Five Primary Vowels are:

1.   EH — As in the word Let

2.   AH — As in the word Hot

3.   EE — As in the word Me

4.   OH — As in the word No

5.   OO — Like in the word You

A great deal of emphasis is placed on vowels for the vocalist because they are the foundation of what we sing. When performing the exercises from *Vocal Insanity*, make sure to follow my guidelines and maintain each pure vowel sound as directed. Besides pure vowels, there also exists *diphthongs*. Diphthongs are two vowel sounds put together to form another vowel sound, such as:

1. **EH and EE** – When they are sung together and slurred, EH first and then EE, they form the A vowel as in the word Wait.
2. **AH and EE** – When they are sung together and slurred, AH first and then EE, they form the I vowel as in the word Time.

You must master each vowel sound and you'll do so in the *Vocal Insanity* exercises. When practicing, maintain each vowel and do not modify them. Personally, I do not ascribe to any sort of vowel manipulation when singing. Meaning I don't change the sound of the vowel to make singing higher easier. Many coaches do and while I understand the principle behind that approach, it's not something I do as a singer or a teacher. The reason being is because I believe a person's individual sound and the way they form vowels is one aspect of what makes a great singer.

Think about how many killer singers with amazing careers have a voice full with character and unique idiosyncrasies. That's the good stuff. The last thing you want to do is mess with that. Unless the technique is somehow dangerous, many times I leave it alone.

As a vocal coach, my job is to hide my work. There's nothing more sterile than to watch a singer who has been over-trained and their coach's philosophy shows everywhere in their singing. Which means to one degree or another, you'll sound like all their other students. Technique strengthens and protects the instrument, but it shouldn't shape a generic, technical tone.

Bottom line; let your tone flow on each vowel as you form it correctly during the exercises, then just sing like there's no tomorrow. With all that's been said over the last five chapters, we've finally reached the trickiest and most misunderstood section for most singers and most vocal coaches-The Rock-n-Roll Sound.

Chapter Six: The Rock-n-Roll Sound

THIS IS THE SECTION LEFT OUT of most voice books, and with reason. Most vocal teachers have no practical experience singing with a dirty, raspy, or crunchy voice. Ask them to sing a tune from *Cats* or *Evita* and they'll bang it out. Ask them to sing, "Welcome to the Jungle," "Smells Like Teen Spirit," or "Crawling" and you'll watch them crawl away in fear. The truth is; most of them can't sing with rasp. I can and have been doing so for many years and I still have a healthy voice. Anyone who tells you that singing rock music is the same as singing Broadway is full of s**t. It's not!

There's absolutely perfect, technically precise singing and there's incorrect singing where you tear your voice up every time you sing. In the middle lies the key. Singing Rock, Hardcore and Hip-Hop is about splitting the difference. The key is to sing with enough technique to stay strong on the road and survive the demands of being the singer in a band, but not being so technical that you sound too polished. Image what it would sound like to have Celine Dion fronting the band, Garbage. Scary!

I must say again that splitting the difference is the ticket. Developing your pharyngeal voice is what helps your voice withstand the assault from singing rock. If the pharyngeal muscle is weak, it will cause you to slightly pull chest in every song, which will slowly and methodically, over time, destroy your voice.

If you move the vowel up and in too much, meaning the voice gets too dark sounding, (imagine turning the treble off on your stereo) as you go up in pitch, it will make your voice sound contrived. It will give you too "warm" a tone (also referred to as a covered sound) and your plea will not cut through to the audience.

Think of the tone of someone trying to jokingly sound like an opera singer. They contrive up the sound and make it sound over-chesty and fake. It's not too pleasing to the ears. To fully understand this concept you need a quick lesson in sound design.

In sound, there is what is known as bandwidth. Bandwidth represents the EQ (equalizer) area that a note is in. Look at a stereo. If it has a ten-band EQ, with each of the EQ faders controlling a few different notes. The EQ faders to the left are for the low notes and the notes it controls get higher as you go to the right. The problem in singing rock is in being heard. The reason being heard can be a problem is because the guitars sit in the same EQ bandwidth as the vocalist, creating a sonic war for first place.

In a band situation, the guitars are processed and compressed. Compression tightens the sound and puts it out in front in the mix, making it easier to hear. If your voice is too wide sounding or too "covered" sounding, it will never be heard and you will be stuck at your day job. The bottom line is you need to cut through and be heard over the guitars that are sitting right on your head in the mix!

The standard "perfect technique" warrants you to move the vowel in too much for rock-n-roll, yet moving it out and pulling chest can tear your voice to pieces. So here is where we split the difference. Move in enough to keep a healthy voice, but not so much that you get lost in the mix. Getting lost in the mix causes singers to over-sing to be heard and is a main cause of vocal problems.

So in a nutshell, moving the voice to "up and in" can cause too warm a sound that doesn't cut and you will be drowned out by the guitars. Letting it flail out can cause hoarseness. What do I mean by "up and in" and letting the sound "flail" out? If you allow the voice to go up and in, the sound will become warmer as you go up in pitch, retaining its tone and resonance. Your voice flails out when you allow the tone to become bright and brittle at the top notes, losing all its tone and resonance.

Again, the secret is to split the difference. Splitting the difference is a term you will become very akin to. The key to splitting the difference is the *Vocal Insanity* exercises, which are designed to help you to achieve that perfect balance.

When you split that difference, you'll produce the pharyngeal tone. Developing a strong pharyngeal voice will enable you to skate the corners and put scream in your voice. Remember, Rock, Hardcore and Hip-Hop music came out of pain, and you need to be able to unload that pain on your audience. If you have a tender voice, you're stuck.

I hope you are excited because we're almost to the exercises. I do ask that you think about what you've learned so far, because when you begin the *Vocal Insanity* exercise program, you must sing hard and mean it. Singing hard isn't going to ruin your voice. As long as you sing correctly, singing hard will only make your vocal muscles stronger!

It may take time to develop that killer sound, but stick at it. If any of the audio exercises starts to cause you problems, stop the exercise. Email me immediately at james@jameslugo.com. The pharyngeal muscle develops slowly, so be patient and don't overdo it. Are you ready to develop that killer voice? Well, we're almost there, just hang with me for a few more chapters, where I'll share some of my favorite performing and recording tips as well as discuss the dos and don'ts of *Vocal Insanity*. Let's move on to some of my best "tricks of the trade."

Chapter Seven: Tricks of the Trade (Stage & Studio)

THOUGH YOU'VE LEARNED QUITE a lot about the voice and you're geared up to start your training, I knew this book wouldn't be complete without sharing some of the best tips I've learned over the years from singing and teaching. Following are the tricks I use for both stage and studio. Many of the tips for stage also apply to studio and vice versa.

Tricks for the Stage

❖ One of the most important things when it comes to singing on stage is to be prepared. First, know your material. If you're doing a quick one-off gig and you're not fully prepared, have good cheat sheets for the stage floor with little phrases or a word that will help you to remember where you are in the song.

❖ Don't show up last minute for the gig. There's nothing more unnerving than jumping on stage at the last minute with a concert hall full of fans, only to realize there are no monitors or the battery in your wireless microphone is dead.

❖ Always have water on stage.

❖ Make sure you are as happy as possible with your stage mix during sound check. Monitor mixes can be less than inspiring at times. Have the mix that makes you comfortable so you can do your best.

❖ Always tip the soundman at sound check. Trust me!

❖ Be careful of starting a show with your hardest or highest song. Even if you've properly warmed up, you should still give yourself the chance to get the flow going.

❖ Speaking of warming up, ALWAYS warm up before a show.

❖ Don't eat two hours before call time.

❖ Always have fun!

Tricks for the Studio

❖ Be prepared. The studio is where the rubber meets the road and can be very humbling for a half prepped singer. Know your words and cues. Have notes and lyrics.

❖ Always bring two copies of the lyrics to every session- one for you and one for the producer/engineers.

❖ Microphone, microphone preamp and compressor selection is crucial and usually the job of the engineer, but it's good to know what you like. Maybe bring in a reference CD of some artists that you like the sound of the vocal recordings as a jumping off point.

❖ Always come to the studio warmed up and have plenty of water.

❖ Wear comfortable shoes and clothes. Don't wear loud, noisy jewelry that the microphone can pick up.

❖ Make sure you like your headphone mix and the lighting in the booth, because they are two very important things for the overall vibe. Personally, I don't like the vocals too loud in relation to the music in my headphones. I like to have to reach a bit when singing. Sometimes having the vocal too loud in the headphones can make a singer sing tentative. If a singer isn't used to hearing their voice that loud in their ears, it can freak them out.

❖ Find a good place for you to have your mouth in relation to the microphone. You may have to back up slightly as you sing higher because you may get louder. This is where you need to be careful, because pulling back too far can thin out the voice on the recording. Likewise, don't move in too close to the microphone or you'll kick in the proximity effect. Basically, your voice has more of the low end when it's closer to the microphone, hence it sounds warmer and fatter when closer.

That's it for tips. Short and sweet; that's how I roll. Honestly, the more you sing and perform the more tips you'll discover on your own. Now, we're almost to the exercises, but let's cover some dos and don'ts before we start exercising.

Chapter Eight: Dos & Don'ts

THERE ARE SOME REALLY GOOD things to do for yourself to help you on your journey as a singer. Here is my list of Dos and Don'ts, stripped down to the bare minimum. Forgive me for not elaborating, but there's no reason for me to do so. Just follow this list and your voice will thank you.

Dos

❖ The most important dos for singers are sleep and water. Your voice is a muscle group. Just like working out at the gym, you'll need rest to repair the muscles. Eight hours of uninterrupted sleep will do more for the health of your voice than anything. Drink a gallon of water each day. You'll be peeing like a racehorse, but you'll also sing like an angel.

❖ Vitamin E helps to keep your voice lubricated, as does a tablespoon of Flaxseed Oil in the morning. Tastes a little nasty but it's like putting a quart of oil in your car. Vroom Vroom!!!

❖ Eating healthfully is critical. Be careful of dairy and citrus, as they create phlegm and make singing difficult.

❖ A steady workout at the gym rocks the voice. Cardio, abdominal crunches, and weights are great for a singer.

❖ Be sure to rest your voice (quit talking) if you know you have something important to sing for and you need to sound your best. On the day prior to the gig, take it easy at rehearsal.

❖ *WARM UP BEFORE REHEARSALS, GIGS & THE STUDIO!*

Don'ts

❖ Things to watch out for are drugs and alcohol. Not only have they taken some of our greatest singers out of our world, they can also destroy your voice.

❖ Smoking. If you do it, stop it! Smoking isn't the secret to a raspy voice. It's the way to lose your voice.

❖ Be careful about singing along with other artists that are vocally out of your range, completely different tonally, or use more rasp than your present ability will warrant. To thine own self be true!

The world has a surplus of bad singers and it doesn't need any more, so don't be one. Take this book and run with it. There is no mistake that you found this book, so take it as a blessing and consider yourself loved. Time for some exercises...

Chapter Nine: Vocal Insanity Exercises

ALAS WE ARRIVE TO THE VOCAL building section. The exercise section is designed to explain the techniques used on the audio portion of the book to help you achieve the greatest results. I will explain them to the best of my ability here in the book, but I also go into detail on the audio.

NOTE: To get your free audio files, go to:

www.venderapublishing.com/LugosInsanityWorkout

Use this chapter as a guideline, but refer to the audio portion daily as some of the exercises are much easier explained by hearing as opposed to reading. Nevertheless, here is a simple breakdown of each exercise:

Exercise Series #1 - Lip and Tongue Rolls

These exercises are the best way to warm up the voice. Each sound enables you to pass over your bridges and breaks without having to form a vowel. They are similar to a runner walking or jogging a few laps before pouring on the mojo. It's good for your voice to warm up slowly. To create the lip roll, let the air pass through the pursed lips and they'll bubble via the air. Some people can lift up their jaws a bit with their hands by placing the fingers at the corners of the mouth to help the lips roll. Tongue rolls occur by fluttering the tongue. Not everyone can do a lip or tongue roll, so if you can't, just hum the scales until you learn. The key to this exercise is to keep the lips or tongue loose and try not to let the voice flip into falsetto as you go up.

Keep the sound in your true voice and allow the tone to stay connected over the break area. I go into greater detail on the track.

Exercise Series #2 - The Vowels

This is an overview of the primary vowels I like to work on. Vowel exercises give you a chance to start singing and get the mechanism moving. We go over basic structure while still allowing the singer to retain their true sound. I am not trying to get you to sound like me or anyone else. The key to all of this is to find your own voice. The vowels addressed are:

AH - like the word 'HOT'
EH - like the word 'LET'
AW - like the word 'AWESOME'
OO - like the work 'YOU'
EE - like the word 'ME'

Exercise Series #3 - EEEYYAAAAH

This is one of my all-time favorite exercises. It does amazing things for increasing vocal range and building intensity. Basically, you start on an EE vowel and as we scale up, then shift to a YAH vowel while dropping the jaw. It trains the voice to open up as you go up in range. The higher range is an area where many singers struggle because many allow excess tension to creep into the vocal muscles, causing them to close up and impede vocal cord function. This exercise addresses this issue and hits it head on with amazing results. Again, I go into more detail on the audio.

Exercise Series #4 - Tongue Out

Another amazing series of exercises and an extension of the EEEYYAAAAH exercises are the tongue out exercises. Singing with the tongue out trains the vocalist to stay open as they ascend, placing emphasis on the vocal cords staying connected, while producing a gutty tone. For R&B singers, this exercise can aid in the gruff sound on riffs and runs. For rock singers, this exercise is like putting high test gas in the engine. It really helps you to sing high and add some grit or scream if you want. I also combine this with the EE vowel on the audio for the full blown effect. Killer technique!

Exercise Series #5 - Staccato

Staccato is Latin for 'short'. These exercises train the vocal cords to open and close quickly and fluidly, which is very important in sounding like a pro. Nothing sniffs out an amateur faster than swooping and sliding all over the place. This trains you to initiate pitch, tone, and intensity instantaneously. This is an invaluable section and I do go into more detail on the audio. I also connect this with singing like you speak and speaking like you sing. Good stuff.

Exercise Series #6 - Pharyngeal & Warm Down

The scales and techniques as applied to the pharyngeal muscle and are a bit of an enigma for many, more misunderstood than understood. I go through the basics of how to train this part of the voice, using slides and cackles. Again, this is best understood via the audio. These exercises can be very intense for some people so they are best done only a few minutes at a time. At the end of the pharyngeal section I go into a short warm down, (also known as a cool down) which is a very good thing to do after the witches cackle.

Exercise Series #7 - Wrap Up

This is not really an exercise section. It's some of my thoughts on how to improve based on my twenty-five years of teaching and singing.

And that finishes *Vocal Insanity*. Reread the book to make sure you understand the voice and begin practicing the exercises every single day to skyrocket your potential. Remember, your voice will be insane if you practice! If you need more guidance, check out my instructional video, *James Lugo's Vocal Asylum*, which is available at:

http://www.groove3.com/str/vocal-asylum.html

I also teach via Skype or live in person in Raleigh, North Carolina. Many people have flown in to study with me from around the world. In my studio, I not only teach voice, but I'm a record producer, mixer, and songwriter as well. Shoot me an email at james@jameslugo.com to inquire about my services and to book a voice lesson. Or visit JamesLugo.com to learn more. To finish out the book, let's move on to some Q&A.

Chapter Ten: Lugo's Q&A

THANKS FOR READING. But before I let you go, I felt this book wouldn't be complete without a little Q&A. Following are some of the best questions I've received and answered over the years:

From Boston Mass-I started a band two months ago...

Q: Will taking singing lessons ruin my ability to sing rock?

A: Not if you get the right coach. The right coach will unlock your true potential - a true coach will bring out your voice - they won't try to teach you how to sing in a contrived voice. A good coach will bring out whatever's there. That, to me, is critical for teaching people how to sing rock. The goal is to keep a singer really grounded in the way they speak. That's how you keep that raw, urban tone which is critical for selling records. Forcing a vocalist to use 'perfect' vowels, ala Latin tongue, and not allowing them to morph the sound a bit to suit their natural voice will give them to polished a sound for rock and ultimately move them away from the goal. Imagine Julie Andrews fronting Metallica. Yuk!

From Portland Oregon-I'm 17 and...

Q: I don't have a high voice. Can you teach me to sing high?

A: Usually when people come to me and say they don't have a high voice, it's just because they don't know how to access their bridges - they don't know how to sing through their range. You probably have plenty of range; you just don't know how to utilize it. That's where the scales, arpeggios and the techniques that we teach at Vocal Asylum come in- what they do is they give you increased range and intensity. Not only do they give you a higher range, but also they give you the ability to sing with some muscle in your upper register instead of sounding flowery and thin, watery or wimpy. You'll have a good solid crank in the upper register of your voice, which is critical for today's music, whether it's dance, rock, metal, hip hop - you know, it doesn't matter, it's all basically the same.

Cheryl from Philly, PA...

Q: What is the difference between a classically trained voice and a rock voice?

A: I feel their design is a bit different. A classical singer is designed to be heard in a large auditorium over a pit orchestra. It's the same thing with musical theater. Back in the day, they didn't have PA systems, so you had to sing over the top. So they had to teach you - your whole body- how to make a big sound so you could be heard. Today's rock's not like that. When you listen to a Mariah Carey album or Linkin Park cd, all you're hearing is what that singer sounded like at the moment they cut the vocal track, one inch away from their lips, the size of a quarter, because of the diaphragm, which is what picks up the sound on the microphone. The diaphragm on a microphone is only like the size of a quarter and it sits about an inch off your lips - that's all the person is hearing. What I try to do is get the singer to take all their energy and get it coming out of the mouth. A hundred percent of your energy focused, compressed and tight, coming out of your mouth, over your tongue and through your teeth, which is a little bit different than classical, because we (rock singers) are amplified and that's the nature of our beast. And I don't believe I want any of my energy being disbursed. It's not picked up in a dispersed manner; it's being picked up in a focused way, right in front of your mouth.

Trevor from Cal State University Student ...

Q: When I sing on stage, I can't hear myself. What can I do?

A: Voice lessons help you to sing with what's known as placement - you start to feel what the notes feel like. That can really help, because sometimes you can't hear yourself. Stage volumes will differ. If you're touring and you're not a high-budget tour, when you go into different towns, you don't know who you're going to have running sound; the equipment doesn't always work and monitor mixes are not always good. But if you learn the placement, meaning, you know what a 'G' note feels like, it helps you to lock in on stage, whether you can hear yourself or not. If you can hear yourself, it's always better, but it's not always the case and that's the whole thing with singing on tour and singing rock and roll. You have really got to be able to adapt. You've got to be flexible and you've got to be able to think on your feet. Because people that go on the road and think they're going to bring some little rigid box of ideas that "this is the way it is" are going to be in for a rude awakening because it's just not. It is what it is. And sometimes you can't hear yourself. But if you've got good placement - like if you really know what the notes 'feel' like, it does help you sing more in tune. Instead of just having to hear the 'G', if you know what a 'G' feels like physically - where it resonates - where the placement of the larynx rest - where everything sits when you hit that 'G',, it makes it a lot easier to hit it if you can't hear yourself that well.

Terry from Los Angeles, CA...

Q: I love singing rock! I saw you play at Paladinos in Los Angeles. Hearing you sing made me start taking my singing seriously. You were very cool for talking to us that night. Sometimes I feel self-conscious when I sing in front of people. What can I do to overcome it?

A: Don't take yourself so seriously. Learn your craft and enjoy it. Usually people get self-conscious because they don't know the material - they don't have their chops together. So maybe you have to go down to the basement and build the monster first or maybe you just need plenty of stage experience. If you're not used to getting up in front of people, Karaoke is a great way to build confidence. If you're a serious singer and you want to get into the Karaoke circuit, I'd go buy a Shure SM-58 microphone. Bring it with you because you don't want to be singing on a microphone that ninety drunks with the flu are drooling on. Bring your own microphone. It's a good way to cut your teeth and stay healthy. Also, start to associate with other singers you know. Sometimes good singers go to Karaoke bars. You'll see people that are into singing and you'll start to run with the crowd. By the way, glad you made it to the gig.

Bryan from Christianstad, Sweden...
Q: I tried out for a band and was told my voice doesn't sound rough enough for rock. But I really want to sing rock. Is there something I can do to get a real rock voice?
A: Yeah - buy a bottle of Jack Daniels and move to LA! Seriously though, that approach has worked for many singers, but it has also ruined a lot of careers. Trust me, I know that one first hand...I've developed a few techniques that help give the voice a raw, meaner sound. Nothing takes the place of the nature of the beast. Rod Stewart was designed to sing like Rod Stewart. When I first started singing I saw this band called World War III - the singer, Mandy, really had that Brian Johnson, ACDC scream down. And this was when I first started singing. I went back stage and started talking to him after the show. I asked him, "How do you sing like that?" And he said, "It's the nature of the beast." Because that kind of singing was what he felt. It's how he expressed himself. You know what I mean? When I met him I had a very clean voice. I had to develop a rough sound - I had to do it through training. For some people, it's natural. For others, it's earned. Either way, it's obtainable. By the way Yngwie's alive and kickin' and residing in Miami.

Rikki from Issaquah, Washington ...
Q: What kind of breathing exercises should I be doing?
A: My belief is that it's returning to childhood as far as breathing goes. It's just back to a natural state of belly breathing. The key to breathing is to lower the origin of your voice. The deeper you breathe, the bigger your voice. It's simple, very simple. When you inhale, for singing, it's like filling up a glass of water. Put it under the faucet - it fills from the bottom up, very simple. The deeper you breathe, the more resonation you're going to have. If you look at an acoustic guitar, what is it? It's an enclosed chamber with a hole in it. You look at a singer - it's an enclosed chamber with a hole in it - the mouth. The deeper you breathe, the bigger the guitar. It's that simple.

From New York City, New York...

Q: I have pitch problems that I'd like to correct. What can I do for pitch problems?

A: A lot of times stuff like pitch problems and vibrato are a result of poor singing technique. If you've got good technique, you've got good posture, you're singing correctly, you've got a good balance between tightening the belly, throat relaxed, air pressure - usually that knocks out most of the pitch problems. Most people that come in here with pitch problems don't always have a problem hearing the note. It's not that they're not good musicians. It's that they're just not playing their instrument right. And that's why they're having pitch problems. So, usually when someone comes to me and says they're having pitch problems, that's a symptom of something else that's going on. A lot of times, something as simple as a tight jaw or bad posture will make a singer flat - Tongue curling back in the mouth will make a singer flat too. Blowing too much air can make a singer sharp. So, usually when it comes to pitch problems, it's just about working with the singer to develop some good fundamentals. another thing you can do if you do have pitch problems is invest in a $99.00 keyboard that has a good piano sound on it where you can shut off the chorus and reverb on it, and there's nothing to make the pitch oscillate or bend. Hit the keys for a straight pitch and just sit there and match each pitch. Hit that middle 'C' and hit an 'AH' and listen to it oscillate in sync. Notes are made from what's known as cycles. An 'A' on the guitar string - the fifth string - is called 'A440' because it cycles at 440 cycles a second. It's like spinning. Think of the kid spinning a rope and the faster he spins it, the higher the pitch. That's kind of a primitive way to look at it, but it works. So think of it - the note is cycling at 440 cycles a second- if you come and you try to hit the note and you're cycling at 432 cycles a second, the sprockets are not going to line up. It's going to sound like a car with a flat tire. It's going to have a wobble in it. You get the keyboard, sit and sing with it and micromanage your voice. Self-awareness of this is critical. The keyboard is really good for eliminating pitch problems.

John from Florida...

Q: I'm learning about belly breathing. It seems that when I do it, more air comes out and less sound comes out when I sing.

A: If that's what's happening, then somebody taught you the wrong way. So you need to get with somebody that can help you with that because the belief is, when you inhale down deep, you use your abdomen to support your voice like a pillar supports an overhang or a loft or something. The pillar doesn't push the thing up, it just doesn't allow it to fall - it supports it. That's what you're supposed to be doing - you're not supposed to be shoving air through it. Good singing is very natural. Once you get accustomed to it, it becomes quite easy. Pushing too much air can destroy your voice!

From Charleston, SC- My name is Peter. You rock dude!

Q: At band practice I get a lot of sore throats. It seems to happen all the time. What causes it and what should I do?

A: There are quite a few things for that. Usually what causes that is pushing too much air and trying to sing too loud over your band if you don't have much of a PA - you gotta be careful. Remember, regardless of what your band thinks, you're the centerpiece of your band if you're singing contemporary music. Your band has to cater to you. The band is usually boxed into the limitations of the singer, bottom line. Your instrument is a one shot deal. You can't throw it down a staircase and go to Guitar Center and buy another voice. You ruin it - it's done. Things that are really good are sleeping with warm mist humidifiers, drinking plenty of water, taking long hot showers, green apples, multi vitamins, vitamin E, getting plenty of rest - uninterrupted sleep and warming up with your practice tape before rehearsal. Of all of it, probably warming up and sleep are the most important. If you're working with a coach now, he or she probably gives you a tape of your lessons and it's probably got twenty to forty minutes of scales and arpeggios. If you run that tape for ten or fifteen minutes before a rehearsal that usually helps. Watch your volume. Because rehearsals in little rooms can get really loud and you'll end up screaming over the band and that causes problems.

Hi, I'm Pamela and I'm working with your tape. It's invaluable...

Q: What is Vegas Throat?

A: It's an old expression - it's basically when singers get stuck in a dry climate. There's no humidity. It's notorious in Vegas - like a singer will be touring and doing great and they go to Vegas and they can't sing anymore. No humidity in the air, high altitudes, and warm temperatures kill your voice. When the vocal cords get dehydrated, they become less flexible and flexibility is critical to the top end of a singer's voice. Take hot showers, use a warm mist humidifier, and drink plenty of water, take your vitamins and rest. Vitamin E and flaxseed oil helps with that too. Keep up the good work with the tape.

Randy Sewell from Austin Texas...

Q: What should I do if I forget the words while I'm singing?

A: Mumble in key, lol.

Dean from Little Rock...

Q: Is it good to have a vocal coach in the studio while I cut my demo?

A: A trained, objective ear in the studio is immeasurably good. It can really make a difference. It's not for everybody. Sometimes it's not in your budget. Sometimes it doesn't suit the person who may want to just vibe out and do their own thing. But I've seen miraculous things done by vocal coaches. I've done some things to help students in the studio, and I've had vocal coaches help me in the studio. I think it's great, personally. Right now I'm finishing my CD, *Redemption* and I'm working with two coaches and my producer, Brian Levi. And we're really dialing this thing in. So it's all up to the individual - plenty of guys go in without vocal coaches and win Grammys and then there's guys that go with vocal coaches and do nothing. So it's up to the individual - I like it personally, as long as the vocal coach isn't very intrusive, not trying to manipulate or change me or make me into something I'm not. That's not good vocal coaching. Good vocal coaching is learning how to bring out the best in the singer. Not changing them and turning them into what you think they should be. Just enhance what's already there.

James from Ohio...

Q: I am recording my demo. But the microphone is distorting. I don't know if it's the compressions setting or microphone placement or preamp. Could you give me a few tips on a home studio setup for rock vocals?

A: When you are getting distortion when recording vocals it can be a few situations contributing to it, here are a few things to try. First, especially if using a condenser microphone, make sure the microphone is NOT perfectly vertical to the ground. Meaning you want to make sure that the diaphragm on the microphone is not perfectly parallel with your mouth. Hitting the diaphragm too square with sound waves and air can cause it to distort, so sometimes a good thing is to hang the microphone upside down with the top of the head basket (which is now closest to the floor) even with your top lip. The diaphragm is slightly above your mouth, where we want it. Now take the head of the microphone and tilt it up and back about an inch, giving a slight angle. The voice will now be recorded without the diaphragm being directly hit with the sound blast. Also check and see if there's a PAD on the microphone and/or microphone preamp. This PAD will lower the volume usually -10db or -20db, which can also really help. Experiment with engaging the PAD. Another trick is mouth distance and microphone technique, mouth distance meaning how far you are from the microphone. Too close can cause distortion, but too far can make the voice sound thin due to proximity effect. Find the right balance and always test microphone volume with the loudest section of the song. And lastly is microphone technique. That is the act of moving closer to the microphone on quieter section and backing off when you get loud of scream. Again proximity effect will play a part. You will get more low end in the voice the closer you get to the microphone and vice versa. So experiment and see what works best for you and the song. This topic in and of itself could be a book. Recording in the studio in an art and can take some time, direction, and trial and error to master.

I hope the Q&A section answered any lingering questions. As I bid you farewell, remember, singing should be fun, so don't take it all so serious. Learn how to laugh and your voice will thank you for it. To put you in the happy zone, here are a few jokes to get you started:

How many singers does it take to screw in a light bulb?
One, they hold the light bulb and the room revolves around them...

How can you tell when a singers lying?
Their lips are moving...

What do you call a singer without a girlfriend?
Homeless...

How do you get a singer off your doorstep?
Pay for the pizza...

How do you know when a singer who thinks he's a drummer is at your door?
The knock speeds up...

Last but not least...*How many guitarists does it take to screw in a light bulb?*
One to screw in the light bulb and ten to say they can do it faster...

I hope you enjoy and benefit from this book; I had a blast putting it together. Good luck.

—James Lugo, Master Vocal Coach, Vocal Asylum

JAMES LUGO'S VOCAL INSANITY

www.VocalAsylum.com
James@JamesLugo.com
818.259.0190

James Lugo's music career spans four decades. After graduating high school in the eleventh grade to pursue college majoring in classical guitar and piano, he landed a tour with an eight-piece jazz band, and went off to see the world. James has done everything from play guitar in Dokken after George Lynch left the band to sing all the Nazareth hits on tour in their original keys with original guitarist Manny Charlton's band. His voice teaching career started in the late 80s as the vocal coach for the Multi-Platinum dance/pop group Expose'. James has worked with a flurry of celebrities over the years as a top Hollywood vocal coach, including Smashing Pumpkins, Flogging Molly and Snoop Dogg and served a vocal coach and voice analyst for American Idol for three seasons. James also is a veteran record producer with a full SSL studio, he offers 'live' online mixing of your record. Check out http://www.SSLMixingOnline.com. Most recently James has been coaching for GLEE and Disney. James' diverse career makes him a wealth of practical knowledge. He only teaches the good stuff. You can learn more about James Lugo at VocalAsylum.com.